SCIENCE AND SOCIETY™

GENETICALLY MODIFIED FOOD

HOW BIOTECHNOLOGY IS CHANGING WHAT WE EAT

Jeri Freedman

ROSEN
PUBLISHING®

New York

To my niece and nephew, Laura and Matthew Freedman,
with love

Published in 2009 by The Rosen Publishing Group, Inc.
29 East 21st Street, New York, NY 10010

Library of Congress Cataloging-in-Publication Data

Freedman, Jeri.
Genetically modified food : how biotechnology is changing what we
eat / Jeri Freedman.
    p. cm.—(Science and society)
Includes bibliographical references and index.
ISBN-13: 978-1-4358-5025-5 (library binding)
1. Genetically modified foods—Juvenile literature. 2. Food—
Biotechnology—Juvenile literature. I. Title.
TP248.65.F66F764 2009
641.3—dc22

                                                          2008013419

Manufactured in Malaysia

On the cover: A researcher checks dishes of experimental plants that
have been grown from lab-cultured cells, into which genetic scientists
inserted new genes.

CONTENTS

G enetically modified (GM) food consists of plants and animals whose genes have been altered. GM food was originally developed to increase the capability of growing certain crops with higher yields as a way to help beat world hunger. A goal of genetic modification is to create crops and livestock that have beneficial characteristics that do not occur naturally in a given species.

GM crops are grown on every continent, except Antarctica. In South America, they are grown in Brazil, Argentina, Uruguay, Paraguay, Colombia, Chile, and Honduras. In Europe, they are grown in France, Spain, Germany, Portugal, Poland, Slovakia, the Czech Republic, and Romania. In Asia, they are grown in India, China, and the Philippines. They are grown in Australia, South Africa, and lastly, North America—Canada, Mexico, and the United States.

The key to genetically modifying food is changing the plant or animal's genes in some way. The nucleus, or center of every cell, contains chromosomes that are threadlike elements that carry genetic information. The chromosomes are composed of deoxyribonucleic acid (DNA). A gene is one segment of a chromosome that determines a particular trait of a plant or animal. Altering a gene will change a specific characteristic of a plant or animal. Changing genes is called genetic engineering.

Genetic engineering has been used to alter animals, including sheep, cows, pigs, chickens, and fish. Genetically modified crops include a variety of foods—rice, corn, soybeans, tomatoes, melons, potatoes, and summer squash, among others—that are eaten around the world.

Throughout the world, the debate still rages over whether genetically modified food is a blessing or a curse. On one hand, genetically modified foods allow farmers to grow crops in places where standard crops won't grow, feeding people and providing income to those in developing nations. They can also reduce people's reliance on dangerous pesticides. On the other hand, there is much that is still not known about such foods. Many people are concerned about genetically modified foods' effects on human and animal health, the environment, local econ-omies, and biodiversity (the number of species that exist).

Rice genes are being mapped at the International Rice Research Institute in the Philippines, one of the many biotechnology laboratories researching genetically modified foods worldwide.

Given the explosive growth in the production of genetically modified foods over the past decade, it is likely that they are here to stay. For this reason, it is important to understand the facts about GM foods.

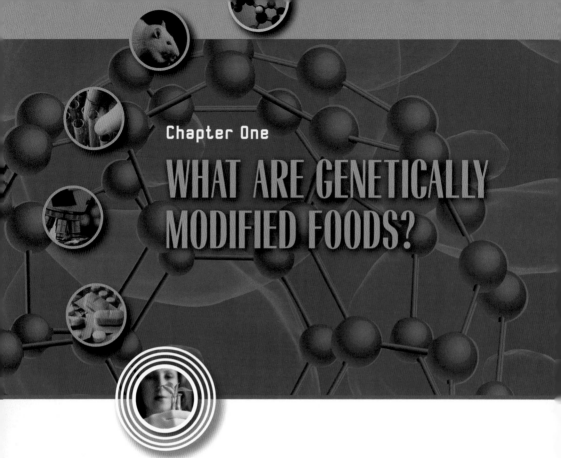

Chapter One

WHAT ARE GENETICALLY MODIFIED FOODS?

G enetically modified plants and animals, often called genetically modified organisms (GMOs), are those whose characteristics have been changed by using modern scientific techniques to add or remove genes. Just what is meant by "genetically modified"? Although this term conjures up images of mad scientists in test tube–filled laboratories, people have had genetically modified food throughout human history.

Genetics is the science that studies how traits, or characteristics, are inherited. "Genetic modification" means changing the characteristics of plants or animals so that they develop new features that people find desirable. For instance, GMOs may be

The nontransgenic corn root *(right)* shows significant damage from the western corn rootworm. The transgenic root *(left)* has much less damage.

able to grow in areas where the soil is too dry for conventional crops to grow.

Sometimes, GMOs are given genes from a different species to provide them with a characteristic from that species. For example, a gene from a bacterium has been used to give corn protection from insects. GMOs modified with genes from another species are called transgenic plants or animals. "Transgenic" means "having genes that crossed over from other species."

History of Modifying Food

The desire to produce better plants and animals has existed as long as people have been growing food. Since ancient times, farmers have practiced a basic type of genetic engineering. If you look at wild species of plants such as corn or blueberries, then you will see that their fruit is much smaller than that of varieties sold in your local grocery store. The reason for this difference in size is that for centuries farmers have sought to improve the size (and other characteristics) of the crops they grow. This allows them to produce a greater volume of food per acre of land, and it provides more food to feed people.

Of course, until the end of the twentieth century, farmers did not have the technology to alter the genes in plants directly. So, how did they go about improving their crops and livestock? They chose the plants with the best disease resistance or largest size, and they saved the seeds from those plants for the next planting. They would pick out the largest cattle or the cows that produced the most milk and breed those animals. So, over time, they produced larger cattle and cows that produced more milk. This approach to modifying plants and animals is called selective breeding. The use of selective breeding dates back to the dawn of agriculture around 10,000 BCE.

Although early farmers figured out how to use selective breeding to improve their crops, they did not know why breeding certain plants or animals together produced specific traits. Therefore, they had to rely on trial and error.

The Dawn of Genetics

It wasn't until the middle of the nineteenth century that people began to scientifically understand how specific characteristics were passed down from generation to generation. The basis for modern genetics was established by Gregor Mendel (1822–1884), a botanist and Augustinian friar at an abbey in Moravia (now part of the Czech Republic). Beginning in 1856, Mendel performed experiments that showed that specific traits of peas, like flower color, could be passed from one generation to another in a predictable fashion. This demonstrated that there was some element that carried information from one generation to the next. Mendel called these information-carrying elements genetic factors.

A historical illustration of Mendel's experiment depicts the distribution of yellow and green peas in three generations. Mendel discovered that the gene for yellow peas was dominant.

Today, they are called genes. (Mendel presented the results of his experimentations in 1865 and published a paper about the plants in the following year.)

Using selective breeding to improve plant or animal species by breeding the best specimens of the preceding generation was not enough for farmers. They sought better ways of improving species—ways that would allow them to create plants or animals with particular traits (characteristics). Their goal was to increase the yield from and maintain quality of crops and livestock.

From the nineteenth century to 1980, scientists and farmers relied on three main methods to improve food species: cross-fertilization, hybridization, and grafting. When botanists (scientists who study plants) or farmers want to improve a type of plant that already exists, they often rely on cross-fertilization. In this approach, they insert pollen from one plant with a desirable trait into the flower of another plant of the same type that also has desirable characteristics. The result is more plants that have the characteristics of the parent plants. Sometimes, a domestic plant with a particular characteristic can't be found. In this case, the domestic plant can sometimes be cross-fertilized with the wild version of that same plant in an attempt to create a domestic plant with the desired trait.

Hybridization takes the idea of combining traits a step further. In hybridization, a new type of plant or animal is created by combining two different species in an effort to combine the qualities of both species. The resulting species will have some characteristics from each of its parents. For example, the loganberry is a hybrid of the raspberry and blackberry, a tangelo is a hybrid of the mandarin orange and the grapefruit, and the beefalo is a hybrid of the American buffalo and a domestic cow.

Grafting is the process of attaching a fruit-bearing sprout of one type of shrub or tree to the trunk of another. Grafting is done for several reasons. In the case of fruit-bearing trees such as apple trees, the fruit-producing species is often grafted onto the trunk of a dwarf (short variety) of tree. Growing apples on smaller trees allows farmers to produce more fruit per acre because the non-fruit-bearing parts of the trees take up less space. Sprouts of hybrid fruits are often grafted onto the trunks of standard varieties because it can take many years for a tree or shrub to reach maturity and produce fruit. However, grafting the hybrid sprout onto a mature plant means that it will fruit in a much shorter period of time. Grafting is also sometimes used when a farmer wants to change the type of fruit grown in an orchard. It is often faster and more cost-effective to graft new stock onto the existing trees than to replant an entire orchard and wait for the new trees to start to bear fruit.

However, one problem with the traditional methods of improving plants is that not every plant can be crossed with every other, even if there is another variety that has a useful characteristic. Another issue is that there is no guarantee that the desired trait will be passed on to every offspring, and it is possible that a negative trait could be passed on along with the desirable one. Thus, scientists set out to find other, more predictable ways of modifying plants.

A Delicious apple bud is being grafted onto a Geneva apple rootstock. In two years, it will develop into Delicious apple–producing branches. This is less time than is needed to grow a new tree.

New Technologies

In the twentieth century, scientists developed new technological approaches to further improve the yield and quality of crops. One such technique is tissue culturing. In tissue culturing, cells or small pieces of tissue are removed from a plant that has traits that are desirable. The tissue is placed in a liquid or solid growth medium along with nutrients and plant hormones (compounds

The Discoveries of Gregor Mendel

Many people consider Gregor Mendel to be the "Father of Genetics." In the mid-1800s, while working with pea plants,

Mendel discovered some of the most important principles that govern inheritance. While at the abbey, Mendel crossbred different varieties of peas. He observed how the parents' characteristics were passed on to their offspring. Mendel studied the plants' height, pea texture (wrinkled or smooth), flower color, and so on. What he discovered was that regardless of which plants he chose as parents, one of three things would occur: all of the offspring would have the same characteristic as one parent (100 percent inheritance); three out of four of the offspring would have the trait (75 percent inheritance); or 50 percent of the children had the same version of the trait as one

Botanist Gregor Mendel's experiments in inheritance with pea plants laid the foundation for the field of genetics.

parent, and 50 percent had the version that appeared in the other parent. From this he deduced that there was some mechanism that controlled how characteristics were passed down from generation to generation. In 1866, Mendel wrote a study of inheritance titled "Experiments on Plant Hybridization." In this work, he coined the term "genetic factor," which was later shortened to "gene." He also noted that a plant or animal could carry a genetic factor that did not affect it but still passed it on to its offspring; for instance, a gene for white flower color in a plant with blue flowers. Scientists now call this a recessive gene. If a gene is recessive, then the offspring must get a copy of the gene from both parents to show that trait. A gene that causes a trait to appear in an offspring, even if it only gets the gene from one parent, is called a dominant gene.

Because Mendel was working in such a remote location, word of his work did not reach Western Europe in his lifetime. Its importance wasn't recognized until his work was rediscovered in 1900 by German plant geneticist Carl Erich Correns, Dutch botanist Hugo de Vries, and Austrian agronomist (a scientist who studies crops) Erich Edler von Seysenegg Tschermak, and translated into English by English zoologist (a scientist who studies animals) William Bateson. It was Bateson who dubbed the study of inheritance "genetics."

that control processes such as growth in a plant or animal). The hormones cause plant tissue to grow into a complete plant, which is an exact copy of the parent plant from which the tissue was taken. The resulting plant is a clone, or identical genetic copy, of the parent plant. Note that no genetic engineering is performed in this basic type of tissue culture. The genetic structure of the plant remains unchanged.

Plants are being grown in test tubes from tissue cultures. These plants are clones of a parent plant and were grown by a form of plant breeding called micropropagation, which uses fragments or cells from the parent plant.

Sometimes, though, there is no existing plant with the exact characteristics that are desired. In that case, breeders try to get the genes in plant cells to mutate, or change, randomly. They hope that in this way a plant with new characteristics may be produced so they can then reproduce the high-quality species. To get the genes to mutate, breeders may expose the plant cells to radiation such as gamma rays or X-rays or treat them with chemicals.

Rise and Fall of a Revolution

From 1965 to 1980, improved fertilizers, pesticides (chemicals that kill harmful plants, animals, or insects), and irrigation (getting water to plants) methods, and scientific plant breeding led to a enormous increase in the yield from many crops worldwide, including such staples as rice and wheat. This era of ever-increasing yields from food plants is referred to as "the Green Revolution." By the mid-1980s, however, it became apparent that the improvements in yield that could be gained from these methods had been exhausted. In addition, getting the maximum yield required very large amounts of chemical pesticides and fertilizers. People were beginning to become concerned about the effects of such chemicals on the environment (in the soil and water) and on those exposed to them. There were still many people in many parts of the world who needed food. Scientists needed either to find a way to increase food production further or to make it possible to grow food in places where it normally would not grow. A new approach was needed.

The Genetic Engineering Era

By the mid-1980s, scientists started to change the genes in cells directly, creating genetically modified organisms (GMOs). There are two main advantages to creating GMOs. First, it takes much of the guesswork out of the breeding process. Instead of mating two plants or animals with desirable traits and hoping the offspring gets the best of both, scientists can choose exactly which traits they want the organism to have. Second, natural change is a slow process. It takes many generations of breeding the best to the best in order to produce significant improvements. The process is much faster if scientists simply alter the genes of organisms so that the organisms possess the trait that is desired.

Genetically Modifying Plants

The first commercial genetically engineered food was the Flavr Savr Tomato produced by Calgene, Inc. It was approved for sale by the U.S. Food and Drug Administration (FDA) in 1994. The

These tomatoes were grown from Flavr Savr seeds. The Flavr Savr tomato was a commercial failure because of its high price and the health concerns about GM food.

Flavr Savr was a delayed-ripening tomato, which means that it could be shipped unripe and it would ripen in food stores. This made it easier to ship and increased its shelf life (how long it would last in stores). Another genetically modified plant was a type of soybean first produced by Monsanto in 1996. The soybean was genetically modified to be resistant to a herbicide used to kill weeds in fields. This enabled farmers to continue to use the herbicide to kill weeds and not soybeans. Soybeans are still one of the most widespread GM crops grown.

Genetically Modifying Animals

In 1987, Harvard University became the first institution to be successful in genetically modifying an animal. The animal was a mouse, which was designed to be used in cancer research. In the past twenty years, more than forty different animals have been genetically modified. These include such food animals as pigs, sheep, fish (like salmon, trout, catfish, and tilapia), beef cattle, and milk cows. In January 2008, the FDA approved the sale of meat and milk from cloned animals. However, at the same time, the U.S. Department of Agriculture (USDA) asked producers to voluntarily refrain from selling cloned meat. In addition, herds of cloned animals would be much more expensive to produce than conventional animals. So, it is likely to be some time before cloned meat appears in stores.

In 1996, scientists achieved success with a new means of genetically modifying animals: cloning. Ian Wilmut and his colleagues at the Roslin Institute in Edinburgh, Scotland, successfully cloned a sheep, which they named Dolly. Dolly was the first mammal to be cloned from a cell taken from an adult animal. In cloning, the nucleus is removed from an egg cell of an animal. The nucleus of a cell from the animal to be cloned is inserted in place of the removed nucleus. The egg is then inserted into a surrogate (substitute) mother and allowed to develop. Although Dolly's healthy birth was greeted with great fanfare in the media, cloning her from an adult cell produced some unforeseen effects. She began to suffer from the effects of old age much sooner than normal. Although she produced a number of

Annie, born in 2000, is the first cloned Jersey cow that was engineered to resist mastitis. Mastitis is an inflammation of the udder, and can cost the U.S. dairy industry more than $1.7 billion annually.

healthy lambs, Dolly lived only six years compared to a typical twelve to fifteen years for most sheep. She has been stuffed and is now on display at the Royal Museum of Scotland.

In addition to genetically modifying livestock directly, scientists have used genetic engineering technology in other ways. Scientists have genetically engineered bacteria to produce compounds that can be used to improve the output of food animals. For example, genetically engineered bovine growth hormone (rBGH) is being produced. Cows injected with this hormone produce more milk than those who are not given the hormone. Injected hormones have become a great concern to consumers, who wonder what the side effects of the hormones might be after eating and drinking these products.

Chapter Two

CREATING NEW FOODS

Scientists create genetically modified organisms by inserting genes into the cells of plants or animals that cause them to develop new characteristics. The genes that are used to alter plants can come from other plants, animals, or bacteria. The genes used to alter animals can come from other animals or human beings.

How Are Genes Modified?

The most frequently used type of genetic engineering is "recombinant DNA technology." "Recombinant" means "recombined" or "mixed." Genes tell the cell what proteins to produce. A protein is a basic

In 2004, the Japanese company Suntory created the world's first blue rose by imserting the gene for blue pigment from pansies into roses.

building block of tissue and substances that control body functions. A combination of proteins results in the appearance of a particular trait. Thus, changing a gene changes a characteristic of the plant or animal. There are three basic aspects to genetically modifying an organism: create a new gene in a form that can be delivered to a cell, deliver the gene to the cell, and grow a new plant or animal that contains the gene.

Scientists first must obtain the gene they want to insert. It can come from another member of the same species they are modifying or from another type of plant, animal, or bacterium. They then insert the gene into the plant or animal they want to

Genetically Modified Food Statistics

According to the International Service for the Acquisition of Agri-biotech Applications (ISAAA), some GM food statistics include the following:

- The number of genetically modified crops worldwide grew 12 percent from 2006 to 2007.
- More than 282 million acres (1,141,214 square kilometers) of land are now used to grow genetically modified crops.
- Twenty-three countries, including the United States, Canada, and Mexico, now grow genetically modified crops.
- Sixty-seven times as many acres were used to grow genetically modified food in 2007 than in 1996, when the ISAAA first started tracking the acreage used.

In Cornell University's Genetically Engineered Organisms Public Education Initiative Project, researchers found:

- 40 percent of the corn grown in the United States is genetically engineered.
- 80 percent of the soybeans grown in the United States are genetically engineered.
- 60 percent of the rapeseed crops grown in Canada are genetically engineered. (Canola oil is obtained from rapeseed and most of the canola oil used in U.S. food products comes from Canada.)

modify, as described in the next section. Sometimes scientists want to change a single characteristic of a plant or animal. At other times, they might change multiple traits at the same time. An organism that has had multiple traits genetically modified is called a "stacked-trait" organism. Monsanto's Roundup Ready/ Yield Guard corn is a stacked trait plant because it is both herbicide resistant and insect resistant.

Methods of Genetically Modifying Plants

With both plants and animals, the key to genetic modification is getting the new gene into the nucleus of the organism's cells, where the chromosomes are located. When working with plants, scientists can start with plant cells, plant embryos (the early stage of a developing plant), or a tissue culture (tiny pieces of plant tissue). Now, it is necessary to get the new gene into the plant's cells.

The most common technique that scientists use to get a new gene into a plant cell is to insert it into a type of bacterium called *Agrobacterium tumefaciens*, which is found in soil. This bacterium is well suited to deliver the gene because it has the ability to insert its DNA into plants. It does this with its own DNA to make plants produce substances that allow the bacterium to survive on them. It is necessary to use the bacterium to deliver the new gene because there are very few things that can penetrate the membrane that surrounds the nucleus of the cell where the chromosomes are located. Once the bacteria have inserted the gene into the plant cells, the cells, embryo, or tissue is cultivated until it produces a viable plant. The new plant will have the inserted gene in all its cells. In most cases, the seeds of the new plant will contain the new gene as well.

Another method of getting a new gene into plant cells is biolistics. This method uses a device called a Biolistic Particle Delivery System, or just a "gene gun," because tiny particles are shot into cells with this method. In biolistics, tiny particles of tungsten, silver, or gold are coated with a liquid containing the gene to be delivered. The particles are then shot into plant cells or plant embryos in a sample dish. The particles carrying the gene penetrate the nucleus of the cells.

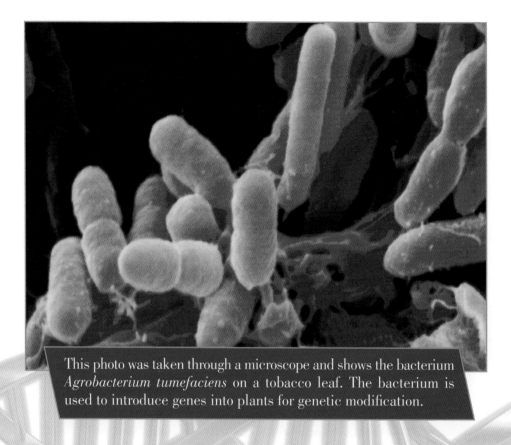

This photo was taken through a microscope and shows the bacterium *Agrobacterium tumefaciens* on a tobacco leaf. The bacterium is used to introduce genes into plants for genetic modification.

Scientists sometimes deliver a "marker gene" along with the active gene that they want to insert. This allows them to verify that the new gene has been successfully incorporated into the plant's DNA. For example, a gene that makes a plant resistant to a herbicide may be combined with a gene that makes a plant resistant to an antibiotic that would normally kill its cells. Once all the genes have been inserted into all the cells, the cells are exposed to the antibiotic. The antibiotic kills the cells that have not taken up the new gene. Those that have taken up the new gene survive because they are resistant to the antibiotic.

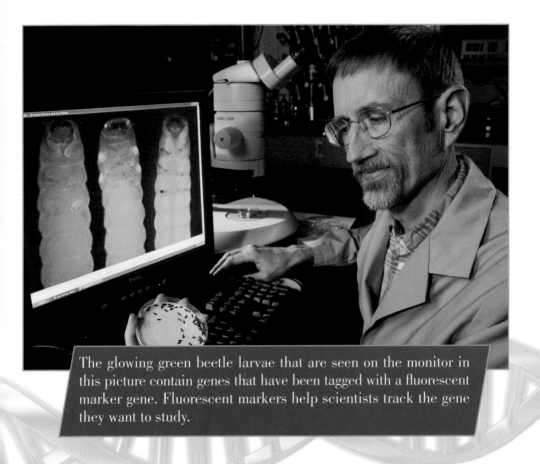

The glowing green beetle larvae that are seen on the monitor in this picture contain genes that have been tagged with a fluorescent marker gene. Fluorescent markers help scientists track the gene they want to study.

Genetically Modifying Animals

A technique called microinjection is the key to genetically modifying animals. Scientists remove fertilized egg cells from an animal and then use a tiny syringe to insert new genes directly into the cells. The eggs are then implanted into a surrogate mother animal. The eggs then develop into normal baby animals that carry the new gene.

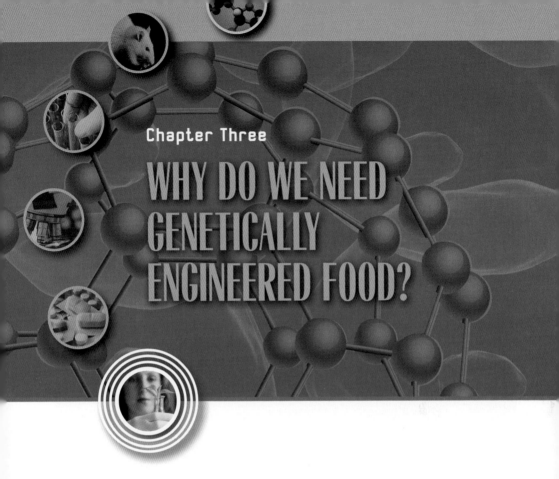

Chapter Three

WHY DO WE NEED GENETICALLY ENGINEERED FOOD?

G enetically modifying foods has the potential to improve people's lives in numerous ways. The keys to providing affordable food for everyone are improving the yield of crops, protecting them from destruction, and enabling them to grow in areas where it is currently impossible. For example, scientists are attempting to genetically modify plants to allow them to grow in very dry areas. The following sections describe some ways in which plants and animals are being genetically modified.

Protecting Plants

To provide the maximum output from crops, it is important to keep plants safe and healthy. One way

A research scientist from the National Center for Food and Agricultural Policy delivers a lecture about corn damaged by armyworms and corn worms in Florida. A Bt gene was developed to protect corn from these insects.

of doing this is to make plants toxic to insects that would otherwise eat them. The most common way to make plants toxic to insects is by implanting a gene from a type of bacterium called *Bacillus thuringiensis* (Bt). This bacterium produces a substance that kills insects. When an insect nibbles on a plant that has had this gene inserted, the insect dies before it can do serious harm to the plant. An example of Bt corn is Aventis Crop Science's StarLink corn. Some people feel that providing plants with a natural defense against insects is good for the environment because it reduces the amount of chemical pesticides that are used. Other people feel that making plants toxic (poisonous) to insects could have a negative effect on biodiversity (the number of different species in an area) in insects by causing certain species to die off. People also worry that such plants could kill harmless insects such as butterflies or have an effect on human health.

Another major threat to plants is disease. Like people, plants are susceptible to a variety of diseases caused by viruses, bacteria, and fungi. For example, it was a fungus that caused the famous famine in Ireland in the 1840s by wiping out most of the potato crops.

Like people, some plants possess genes that give them resistance to a particular disease. Therefore, one way that scientists can genetically modify crops is by inserting a gene from a disease-resistant plant of the same species. However, scientists are not limited to using genes from the same species. They can insert a gene from another plant or a bacterium. For example, some bacteria make substances that break down fungus cells. Inserting such a gene in a plant can make it produce this substance, which destroys fungus that comes in contact with the plant. Other genes that are being experimented with block substances needed by viruses to reproduce themselves, thus stopping the virus from harming the plant. Making disease-resistant plants guarantees that more plants survive to produce fruits and vegetables, which helps to ensure an adequate food supply. Giving plants natural immunity to diseases could also help protect the environment. Such plants could reduce the amount of chemicals that must be sprayed on them to kill fungus-based diseases and insects that otherwise spread diseases from plant to plant.

Making Fruits and Vegetables Last Longer

One of the major problems faced by food producers and sellers is that a large amount of harvested produce spoils before it is sold. Scientists are attempting to develop fruits such as melons and apples that will ripen without becoming soft. The idea is that such fruits could be left to ripen on the vine or tree so that they have flavor, but they would still be firm enough to ship without being

Two scientists check apples that have been genetically engineered to produce larger than normal amounts of a rot-inhibiting protein. Such fruit should last longer in stores.

damaged. Having such fruits would eliminate the need to pick fruits when they are unripe in order to get them to stores before they soften up. Once picked, fruit does not become any sweeter as it ripens because it ceases to produce sugar. Those in favor of the new technologies feel that they would increase the time fruits last in stores and reduce wastage during shipping. Those opposed to them say that the focus on improving fruits and vegetables should be on giving them better flavor, not a longer shelf life. In

Patenting Food

One of the most controversial issues related to genetically modified food is the right of corporations to patent GMOs. A patent is a legal right that gives ownership of an invention to the person or company that invented it. The owner of the patent has the sole right to produce that invention, and other people can only do so with the owner's permission. Often getting such permission requires paying a license fee. This means that if a company produces genetically modified seed for insect-resistant corn or rice that grows in arid (dry) regions, then the only way that people in poor countries can get that seed is by buying it from the company that holds the patent. Because it holds the patent, the company can charge a lot of money for its seed, making it difficult for the people who need it most to get it. In addition, those opposed to patenting such as Genetic Resources Action International have accused some companies of making genetic modifications to crops that have been grown for generations, like varieties of rice, in an attempt to gain financial control over such crops. Such opponents of patenting claim that it is the farmers themselves, who have cultivated the crops for generations, who are responsible for most of the development of the plants. There have also been cases in which genetically modified crops have unintentionally cross-pollinated with non-genetically modified crops. Some corporations have considered these cases to be patent infringement.

The companies who are developing GMOs say that they need patent rights to make back their financial investment and that giving companies patent rights encourages companies to create new products.

addition, there is the concern that GM fruits and vegetables are not equivalent in vitamins and minerals to non-GM food.

Better Livestock

As with crops, one major goal of genetically modifying animals is to make them resistant to diseases, which can often destroy entire herds. An example of such a disease is hoof and mouth disease, which kills large numbers of cattle and pigs each year. If scientists were able to insert a gene that makes animals resistant to the virus that causes the disease, then this could significantly cut down on losses. Genetic approaches may be feasible for giving

A researcher at Seoul National University in the Republic of Korea shows a cloned cow that has been genetically modified to resist mad cow disease. Eating beef that is contaminated with mad cow disease can cause brain damage.

animals resistance to other diseases as well, like bovine spongiform encephalopathy, which is better known as mad cow disease.

Another area being investigated is ways to make animals produce more and better meat. Scientists are experimenting with modifying animals' genes so that they produce more growth hormone, a substance produced in the body that causes it to grow. Putting out more growth hormone would cause food animals to produce more meat. Another way to produce more meaty animals is being explored in pigs. Sows have been genetically modified to produce milk that is more easily digested by piglets. The piglets absorb more nutrients from such milk and grow larger than piglets that suckle on non-GMO sows. But volume is not the only area being worked on. Scientists are also working to improve the quality of meat. For instance they are experimenting with genetic modification to make animals produce leaner meat by making them grow less fat. Finally, a large amount of genetically modified grains is being put to use as animal feed for conventional animals.

Better Nutrition

Millions of people around the world suffer a lack of necessary nutrients because of limitations on what will grow in their region. One area that scientists are exploring is genetically modifying vegetables to increase their nutritional value.

A plant biotechnologist inspects genetically modified golden rice at the International Rice Research Institute (IRRI) in the Philippines. The IRRI has a gene bank with more than 110,000 varieties of rice.

An example of this is "golden rice." This variety of rice is genetically engineered to produce vitamin A—the vitamin that gives carrots their orange color. A vitamin A deficiency can have serious effects, including blindness and even death. Millions of people suffer from this problem worldwide because they live in areas where vegetables containing the vitamin will not grow. Since rice will grow in these regions, golden rice could provide at least some of this critical vitamin to the local population.

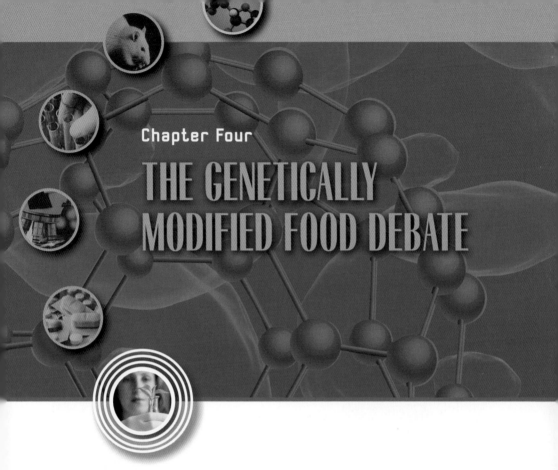

Chapter Four

THE GENETICALLY MODIFIED FOOD DEBATE

F ew subjects have generated as heated a debate as genetically modifying food. The widespread cultivation of genetically modified plants and animals raises many issues for society and the world as a whole.

Effects on Non-modified Plants and Animals

One concern about planting genetically modified plants is that their pollen might spread their genes to nearby fields of non-GMO or wild plants. Another fear is that the gene could spread to other types of plants; for example, a gene for herbicide resistance

An Iowa farmer stands behind a sack of organic corn seed. Many farmers of organic produce are concerned that pollen from GM plants will float over their fields and will contaminate their crops.

might spread to weeds. This process is called out-crossing. So far, there have been few cases of such gene transfers occurring between different species of plants. However, there have been many cases of seeds from genetically modified produce spreading to nearby non-GM crops and wild areas. As GM varieties become more widely grown, people can't be sure that it won't happen.

Earlier, the issue of pesticide-producing plants killing harmless insects was discussed. Another issue related to pesticide-producing plants such as Bt corn is that in the past, whenever a new pesticide has been introduced, insects eventually have developed resistance to that chemical. Just as some plants have a gene that makes them resistant to a disease, some members of the insect population will, by chance, have a gene that makes them resistant to the Bt toxin. Members of the insect population that are susceptible will die off, and those who are naturally resistant will survive and breed. Therefore, it is possible that, if large numbers of a particular species of insect are exposed to Bt corn, then that species will eventually become resistant, eliminating the effectiveness of the Bt toxin.

Biodiversity Issues

Biodiversity refers to how many different varieties of plants and animals exist in a region. Maintaining biodiversity is important because different plants and animals are likely to prosper in different environmental conditions. We do not know when factors such as climate may change. If environmental factors change, then the varieties of plants and animals we rely on may no longer be able to survive or may do so at a reduced level. Having many varieties helps to ensure that we are not reliant on a single source of food that may someday be threatened. The biodiversity of food plants has been decreasing for several decades, as new, higher-producing varieties of food crops have been developed. Some people fear that the widespread planting of genetically modified varieties of crops, with more desirable traits—such as greater

An international seed bank in Mexico City is collecting seeds from every native strain of corn in Mexico. As pests learn to adapt to attack commercial strains of corn, scientists can use the pest-resistant traits of the native strains for breeding purposes so that the commercial strains can be protected.

yields, and drought, disease, or insect resistance—will further reduce biodiversity and significantly alter the food chain.

The Welfare of Animals

Many individuals and organizations that focus on the welfare of animals are concerned that genetically modifying animals may cause them stress and suffering. For example, genetically

Pharming Plants and Animals

Pharming is the raising of plants or animals that produce pharmaceutical products. Research is also being done on genetically modifying animals to produce medications that could be used to treat human diseases. Among the diseases being explored are cancer, heart disease, diabetes, and abnormal blood clotting. Examples include genetically engineered cows that would produce medically useful compounds in their milk and chickens that would produce eggs containing such pharmaceuticals. A second aspect of pharming being explored is genetically engineering plants to produce vaccines to viruses such as HIV (the virus responsible for causing AIDS), hepatitis B, and measles. When nutritional supplements or pharmaceutical compounds are produced in genetically modified plants or animals, they are referred to as "nutraceuticals." Although the fruit, milk, or eggs containing vaccines could easily be processed and distributed to populations at risk, the concept has raised a great deal of controversy. Issues include how to make sure people know that the produce contains a medically active compound, how to ensure that people won't have a bad reaction to consuming it, and how to control distribution so people do not consume too much of the active ingredient. Another issue of concern is how to keep the gene that causes the pharmaceutical to be produced from spreading to other plants or animals, thus contaminating a large part of the food supply.

This transgenic dairy cow produces a substance in her milk that kills the bacterium that causes mastitis. Scientists could use this gene-transfer approach to produce milk that contains other compounds.

modifying animals such as cattle and chickens so that they produce more meat produces larger, heavier animals. This additional weight could cause increased strain on their joints and internal organs, which could lead to painful health problems such as arthritis.

Another concern is that when animals are genetically modified so that they will produce compounds useful for human health, the presence of those compounds in the animals' systems may produce side effects that cause them to develop joint or eye problems, or other serious health problems. There are, however, agencies such as the U.S. Department of Agriculture (USDA) and the American Association for Animal Laboratory Science that regulate and monitor the treatment of experimental animals. A case can be made that the same type of certification and inspection process used to ensure the welfare of conventional animals could be applied to guarantee that any modifications made to animals do not cause them to suffer.

GMOs and Feeding the World

For the past decade, a debate has been raging over whether or not genetically modified food is necessary to solve the problem of feeding people around the world who do not have enough to eat. Some people claim that enough food is produced worldwide by conventional methods to feed everyone. The problem is getting the food from areas that make too much to the areas that make too little. It is true that enough food is produced to feed all the people around the world. However, the majority of food is grown in developed nations with temperate climates such as the United States, Canada, and Europe. Many of those who lack adequate food live in developing nations in places such as Africa. Distributing the excess food grown in food-producing parts of the world to those in areas that need it might be one way of addressing world hunger. Nevertheless, people and companies that have incurred expenses to produce food are not likely to give it away for free. In many cases, though, neither the people nor the governments of developing nations have sufficient funds to buy enough food from developed nations to feed all their people.

Another area of concern is whether the genetically modified crops being grown in developing nations are actually being used to feed people in those regions. The World Trade Organization (WTO) has long encouraged farmers in developing nations to grow crops as a source of income. A large amount of GM crops currently grown in developing nations are actually being sold as animal feed to agricultural companies in developed areas such as Europe and the United States. Although the income from these crops provides farmers with profits, some people believe that more of the crops grown in developing nations should be used to provide food to the local population.

Another objection to a reliance on genetically engineered food is that it creates a reliance on seeds provided by companies that charge for them. Such companies often forbid farmers to save or use seeds from the plants they grow or to breed animals that have been genetically engineered. On one hand, this means that people in developing nations have to keep buying seed instead of being able to save it, potentially giving private companies control over much of the world's food supply. On the other hand, it is true that genetically engineered crops allow food to be grown in regions where conventional crops won't grow, thus feeding people who might otherwise starve. For this reason, the United Nations Human Development Report (UNHDR) has suggested that Third World nations should be allowed to do their own evaluations of the risks associated with genetically engineered produce. They should also decide for themselves whether or not they wish to grow such crops.

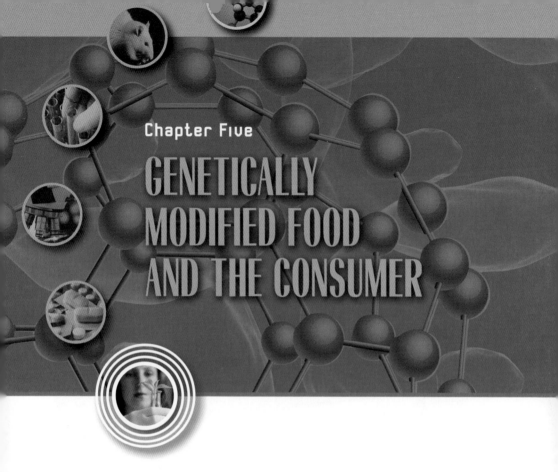

Chapter Five

GENETICALLY MODIFIED FOOD AND THE CONSUMER

G lobal issues are important, but there are many issues related to genetically modified food that strike closer to home. The most important concern is whether genetically modified food is safe to eat. To date, the response of consumers to genetically modified food has been cool—in many cases downright suspicious.

In 2001, the USDA conducted a series of experiments to evaluate consumers' willingness to buy GM food. The study is described in a USDA Technical Bulletin, "The Effects of Information on Consumer Demand for Biotech Foods: Evidence from Experimental Auctions." The USDA selected consumers in two cities in the Midwest and divided

These people hold a rally in the Midwest to protest a cereal company's use of genetically altered crops in its products.

them into three groups. The USDA gave the first group packets with positive statements from authorities about GM food, the second group packets with negative statements, and the third group both positive and negative statements about GM food. They then asked consumers how much they would be willing to pay for various grocery products if they were labeled as being made from conventionally grown food or labeled as containing "biotech" food products. Items included a one-pound (454 grams) bag of corn chips, a five-pound (2.27 kilograms) bag of potatoes, and a thirty-two-ounce (0.95 liter) bottle of vegetable oil.

The study found that consumers' attitudes toward GM food were influenced by the type of information they received about it. When they received only negative information, they were only willing to buy GM food if it cost 35–38 percent less than the conventional product. If they received both positive and negative information, then they would only buy it if it cost 16–24 percent less. When they received only positive information, they were equally willing to buy the GM food or non-GM food. However, the reality is that since concerns about the negative effects of GM food are often reported in the media, most consumers receive at least some negative information about GM food. This makes them less willing to purchase it. There are a number of issues that concern consumers about GM foods.

Is GM Food Safe?

Genetic engineering techniques are not just being used to give a plant or animal a gene from the same species that confers a desirable trait such as larger pea size. Plants are being given genes that cause them to put out toxic compounds that kill insects. Animals are being given genes that make them produce larger-than-normal amounts of growth hormone. One concern is what happens when people eat food containing these compounds. What happens when conventional food animals eat these products and are then sold for food themselves? Will the toxins in the GM animal feed be passed on to the people who eat the meat? Will consuming these compounds affect people's health in ways that scientists don't yet understand? Will the hormones in the animals transfer to humans and what will the effects be?

Another concern is that, in many cases, the genetic engineering process involves inserting in plants a gene that confers antibiotic resistance. If the gene is transferred to people when they eat such food, then it is possible that the gene will also be picked up by bacteria that people come in contact with. If the gene were to spread throughout a population of disease-causing bacteria, then the result might be antibiotic-resistant bacteria, which doctors would have no way to fight. Finally, there is a concern that there might be a higher incidence of food allergy reactions when people eat GM food.

Allergies to GMOs

According to the American Academy of Allergy, Asthma, and Immunology, twelve million Americans suffer from food allergies, including 2.2 million school-aged children. In all, fifty million Americans suffer from allergies of all sorts. Therefore, a major concern with genetically modified foods is that they might cause an allergic reaction in people who eat them. Some allergic reactions are mild, but others can be so severe that they cause death.

A substance that causes an allergic reaction is called an allergen. An allergen could be introduced into a normally safe food when genes of a plant to which a person is allergic are inserted into another kind of plant. A person may be allergic to a substance, like a pesticide, that a plant has been genetically modified to produce. There are currently no requirements in the United States that genetically modified foods be labeled as such—either simply as being GMOs or with a list of genes or compounds they contain. Therefore, people could unknowingly consume such a

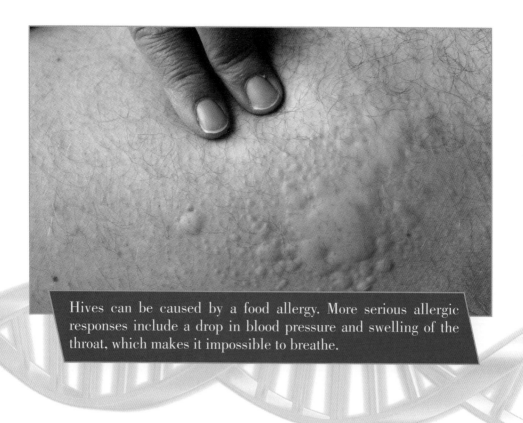

Hives can be caused by a food allergy. More serious allergic responses include a drop in blood pressure and swelling of the throat, which makes it impossible to breathe.

food without being aware that it might cause them to have an allergic reaction to it.

Regulating Genetically Modified Food

In the United States, the FDA, the Environmental Protection Agency (EPA), and the USDA are responsible for regulating genetically engineered food. The USDA oversees the release of genetically modified plants and animals into the environment, whether for field testing or commercial use. The EPA regulates pesticides and pesticidal agents, including plants with pesticidal properties, which may affect plants and animals in the environment. The FDA regulates genetically modified food products that are sold to consumers or mixed into processed foods that are sold

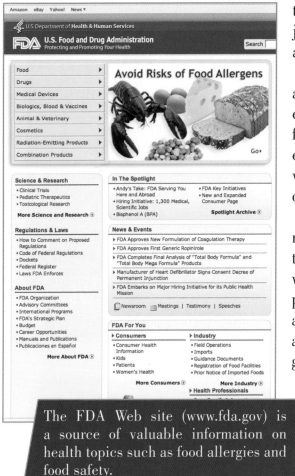

The FDA Web site (www.fda.gov) is a source of valuable information on health topics such as food allergies and food safety.

to consumers. It's the FDA's job to ensure that such foods are safe for people to eat.

In 1992, the FDA issued a policy that stated it considered genetically engineered food to be "substantially equivalent" to conventional varieties of food unless evidence showed otherwise.

In 2006, the FDA implemented a set of guidelines for the evaluation of plants that were genetically modified to produce new proteins such as those with pharmaceutical applications. However, these guidelines apply only to a small number of genetically modified plants that are designed to produce new substances. Concern over the lack of regulation of genetically modified food has led the consumer protection organization the Center for Food Safety to file a lawsuit against the FDA in June 2006. The lawsuit claimed that regulation of genetically modified food is inadequate. It demanded that genetically modified foods be forced to undergo rigorous testing before being approved for sale and that they be labeled clearly when they are sold. At the time of this writing, the suit had not been decided.

In Canada, genetically modified foods are regulated by Health Canada (HC), the Canadian Food Inspection Agency (CFIA), Environment Canada (EC), Agriculture and Agri-Food Canada

(AAFC), and the Department of Fisheries and Oceans (DFO). In 2007, the CFIA started a pilot project called the Biotechnology Transparency Project. As part of this project, CFIA lists on its Web site the genetically modified foods that have been submitted for approval. Both scientists and the general public are invited to submit their comments and concerns, which are then forwarded to HC or the company producing the product to be addressed.

Internationally, government organizations such as the European Union are also actively seeking to regulate and monitor genetically modified food. Because genetically modified food affects people worldwide, there was a clear need for an international organization to evaluate issues related to GMOs. In July 2000, the Codex Alimentarius Commission was formed by the World Health Organization (WHO) and the Food and Agriculture Organization (FAO) of the United Nations. The joint commission issues recommendations and standards for genetically modified food. For example, the guidelines state that governments should test genetically modified foods prior to sale to make sure they don't cause allergic reactions. It also calls for labeling genetically modified foods that might cause allergic reactions. In 2007, the commission began an investigation titled Safety Assessment of Foods Derived from Biotechnology. It is soliciting information from the scientific community on the safety of food made from genetically modified animals.

Labeling Genetically Modified Food

Requiring genetically modified food to be so labeled would at least provide consumers with the option of choosing whether or not they want to eat it. A number of countries have laws requiring the labeling of genetically modified food. These countries include those in the European Union, Australia, Japan, and China. Canada requires the labeling of genetically modified foods that might cause allergic reactions or have a difference in nutritional value from their conventional counterparts. However, in the

This brand of tomato puree is marketed by a British supermarket chain. Unlike the United States, countries in the European Union require food companies to label products that contain genetically modified food.

United States the FDA does not currently require labeling of genetically modified foods. Manufacturers of genetically modified food object to laws being passed that require the labeling of GM food because they fear it will have a negative effect on consumers.

There is, however, a significant problem with attempting to label genetically engineered food. Genetically engineered products, including corn and soybean products and canola oil, are often incorporated into processed food products such as cookies. Sometimes, GM produce is also mixed with non-genetically modified vegetables in canned goods such as tomato paste, which contains tomatoes from many sources. The situation becomes more complicated when the already-combined product is used to make another food; for example, if the tomato paste is purchased in bulk by a company that makes frozen lasagna.

The Future of Food

So far, most genetically modified foods have been modified to produce features of benefit to the companies that produce the seeds

Steven Druker, executive director of the Alliance for Bio-Integrity, has counseled the public about the problems with genetically engineered food. He said that the FDA's own scientists and other experts have warned consumers about the health hazards of genetically engineered food.

(manufacturers), those that grow the food (farmers), or those that sell the food (supermarkets). Nonetheless, genetically modified food could be produced that actually benefits consumers. Genetic modification could be used to create produce that has higher levels of substances that improve people's health. For example, blueberries, tomatoes, and broccoli are natural sources of anti-oxidants (compounds that protect cells from damage). They can help protect people against health problems such as some types of eye disease and cancer. Producing fruits and vegetables with more antioxidants than conventional varieties could help people stay healthier longer.

Vegetables could also be genetically engineered to produce more vitamins. At the very least, produce could be genetically engineered to improve its taste and texture. One possible approach would be to incorporate genes from heirloom varieties of plants (old varieties of fruits and vegetables that are no longer grown commercially). Often, such varieties are no longer grown because they are too small, are an inconvenient shape for packing and shipping, or are too fragile to ship easily. By combining the appealing aspects of heirloom varieties with their hardier relatives, it might be possible to produce tasty varieties that are easy to ship. Some work is starting to be done in this area. For instance, a February 2008 *New York Times* article reported that a company in New Zealand, Crop and Food Research, has succeeded in making an onion that doesn't make people cry when they chop it. Indeed, the key to winning over consumers may be incorporating features into genetically modified food that improve the consumers' experience, not just the manufacturers'.

Despite people's concerns about genetically modified food, more of it is being grown each year. There is little doubt that, in the coming years, plants and animals will be genetically modified in new and different ways. Scientists are experimenting with genetically engineering plants to produce plastics, for example. People need to make sure that they gain a thorough understanding of the effects that raising and consuming GMOs have on both the environment and their bodies.

MYTHS AND FACTS

MYTH   I only eat organic meat and vegetables, so I don't consume any genetically modified foods.

FACT   According to the vice president of the Grocery Manufacturers Association, as quoted in Bill Lambrecht's book *Dinner at the New Gene Café*, as much as 70 percent of processed foods sold in the United States may contain genetically modified food products, so if you eat processed foods like chips or cookies, you could be consuming GM ingredients such as corn, wheat, or soy.

MYTH   Genetically modified foods have reduced the amount of chemicals being used to grow food.

FACT   The widespread use of plants such as Monsanto's herbicide resistant Roundup Ready corn and soybeans has actually increased the amount of chemical herbicide being used to grow crops. These plants make it safe to use such chemicals around widely grown food plants, like corn and soybeans.

MYTH   If the government allows it to be sold, then it must be safe to eat.

FACT   Very little scientific testing has been done on the safety of genetically modified food currently being sold or used in prepared food products.

GLOSSARY

allergen An allergy-causing substance.

antioxidants Substances in plants and animals that help protect human cells from damage.

biodiversity The number of different types of plants and animals in an environment.

biolistics Method of inserting genes into a plant cell by attaching them to metal particles and "shooting" them into the cell.

botanist Scientist who studies plants.

clone A plant or animal whose genetic makeup is identical to that of its parent.

cloning Process in which the nucleus is removed from an egg and is replaced by the nucleus of a cell taken from a parent animal. The egg is then reinserted into a surrogate mother animal and is allowed to develop.

cross-fertilization Also called cross-pollination. Introduction of pollen from one plant into the flower of another plant in order to breed plants with specific traits.

deoxyribonucleic acid (DNA) The material that makes up genes and carries the information that tells cells what substances to produce.

embryo Early stage of a developing plant, animal, or human.

gene A sequence of DNA on a chromosome that codes for a particular trait.

genetic engineering Directly changing the genes of plants or animals to produce specific characteristics.

genetically modified organism (GMO) Plant or animal whose DNA has been directly altered.

herbicide A chemical compound that kills weeds.

hormone A chemical produced in the body that affects the way the body functions.

hybridization Process of combining two types of plants to create a third type of plant that has some of the characteristics of each of its "parent" plants.

marker gene Gene attached to another gene being inserted into a plant cell in order to allow scientists to identify those plants that have incorporated the desired gene.

microinjection A technique by which genes are directly inserted with a tiny syringe into the nucleus of a cell.

mutate To change; this sometimes happens to genes of a plant when they are treated with radiation or chemicals.

nucleus The center of a cell, where the components that contain genes are found.

nutriceuticals Medically beneficial compounds produced in GM plants or animals.

pesticide A chemical compound that kills insects.

pharming Raising genetically modified animals to produce medically beneficial compounds.

protein Basic compound that makes up plant or animal tissue.

recombinant DNA Containing a combination of DNA from more than one source.

selective breeding Choosing specific plants or animals with desirable traits to breed so that subsequent generations will have those traits.

shelf life How long a product lasts before it becomes unusable.

species A group of animals that share common characteristics and can breed among themselves.

stacked trait plant A plant in which more than one characteristic has been genetically modified.

surrogate Substitute; used to refer to an animal into which a genetically modified egg is inserted and allowed to develop.

trait A characteristic.

FOR MORE INFORMATION

Biotechnology Industry Organization
1201 Maryland Avenue SW, Suite 900
Washington, DC 20024
(202) 962-9200
Web site: http://bio.org
This organization provides a wide range of information and
   reports on the application of biotechnology to products,
   including GMOs and GM food and bioethics.

The Center for Food Safety
660 Pennsylvania Avenue SE, #302
Washington, DC 20003
(202) 547-9359
Web site: http://www.centerforfoodsafety.org
This is a consumer advocate organization that seeks to control the
   use of genetically modified foods. It provides a variety of news
   information on the dangers of genetically modified foods.

Council for Biotechnology Information
1201 Maryland Avenue, SW
Suite 900
Washington, D.C. 20024
(202) 962-9200
In Canada:
102-116 Research Drive
Saskatoon, SK
S7N 3R3
(416) 922-1944
Web site: http://www.whybiotech.com
This organization provides scientific information on biotechno-
   logical food and agricultural products.

Council for Responsible Genetics
5 Upland Road, Suite 3
Cambridge, MA 02140
(617) 868-0870
Web site: http://www.gene-watch.org
The council encourages public debate about the social, ethical,
and environmental effects of genetic technologies.

Department of Food Safety, Zoonoses and Foodborne Diseases (FOS)
World Health Organization (WHO)
Avenue Appia 20
GH-1211 Geneva 27, Switzerland
+41 22 791 1067
Web site: http://www.who.int/foodsafety/biotech/en/
FOS works to reduce the serious negative impact of foodborne
diseases worldwide and to ensure a safe global food supply.

Food and Agricultural Organization of the United Nations
Viale delle Terme di Caracalla
00153 Rome, Italy
+39-06-57051
Web site: http://www.fao.org
This organization devoted to addressing world hunger provides a
variety of statistics, and online and written publications on
a range of topics related food issues in countries throughout
the world.

Health Canada
Office of Biotechnology and Science
Health Products and Food Branch
Health Protection Building, Tunney's Pasture
Postal Locator 0702A
Ottawa, ON K1A 0L2
Canada
(613) 597-0362

Web site: http://www.hc-sc.gc.ca
This is the organization responsible for approving genetically
modified foods in Canada. It provides information on GM
food and the regulations that affect it.

Monsanto Company
800 North Lindbergh Boulevard
St. Louis, MO 63167
(314) 694-1000
Web site: http://www.monsanto.com
The premiere manufacturer of genetically modified food, this
corporation provides information on a range of GM foods.

Organic Consumers Association
6771 South Silver Hill Drive
Finland, MN 55603
(218) 226-4164
Web site: http://www.organicconsumers.org
An online nonnprofit group campaigning for food safety, health,
justice, and sustainability. Members focus on promoting the
views and interests of the United States' organic consumers.

True Food Network
The Center for Food Safety
2601 Mission St, Suite 803
San Francisco, CA 94110
(415) 826-2770
Web site: http://www.truefoodnow.org
This is an organization composed of people concerned about the
possible dangers of genetically modified food. It provides
information of activities and legislation related to controlling
genetically modified food.

U.S. Department of Agriculture
1400 Independence Avenue SW

Washington, DC 20250
(202) 720-2168
Web site: http://www.usda.gov
This agency has oversight over both test and commercial genetically modified crops and animals. It provides information on
biotechnology and food.

U.S. Food and Drug Administration Center for Food Safety &
Applied Nutrition
5100 Paint Branch Parkway
College Park, MD 20740
(888) 723-3366
Web site: http://www.cfsan.fda.gov
This organization provides information on food safety issues. Its
biotechnology area provides the latest news related to genetically modified food.

Web Sites

Due to the changing nature of Internet links, Rosen Publishing
has developed an online list of Web sites related to the subject
of this book. This site is updated regularly. Please use this link
to access the list:

http://www.rosenlinks.com/sas/gmf

Barbour, Scott. *Introducing Issues with Opposing Viewpoints: Genetic Engineering*. Chicago, IL: Greenhaven Press, 2005.

Bledsoe, Karen E. *Science on the Edge: Genetically Engineered Food*. Chicago, IL: Blackbirch Press, 2005.

Farndon, John. *From DNA to GM Wheat: Discovering Genetically Modified Food*. Portsmouth, NH: Heinemann, 2006.

Kowalski, Kariann. *The Debate Over Genetically Modified Food: Healthy or Harmful?* Berkeley Heights, NJ: Enslow, 2002.

Morgan, Sally. *Superfoods: Genetic Modification of Foods*. Portsmouth, NH: Heinemann, 2002.

Parker, Steve. *Genetic Engineering*. Chicago, IL: Raintree, 2005.

Rees, Andy. *Genetically Modified Food: A Short Guide for the Confused*. London, England: Pluto Press, 2005.

Siedler, Maurya. *The Ethics of Genetic Engineering*. Chicago, IL: Greenhaven Press, 2004.

Torr, James D. *Genetic Engineering*. Chicago, IL: Greenhaven, 2006.

Yount, Lisa. *Modern Genetics: Engineering Life*. New York, NY: Chelsea House, 2006.

BIBLIOGRAPHY

Agence France-Presse. "New Zealand 'No Tears' Onion." *New York Times*, February 2, 2008. Retrieved March, 24, 2008 (http://www.nytimes.com/2008/02/02/world/asia/02briefs-onion.html?_r=1&ref=science&oref=slogin).

American Academy of Allergy, Asthma, and Immunology. "Allergy Statistics." Retrieved February 28, 2008 (http://www.aaaai.org/media/resources/media_kit/allergy_statistics.stm).

Center for Genetics and Society. "Animal Technologies—Background: Cloned and Genetically Modified Animals." April 15, 2005. Retrieved February 13, 2008 (http://geneticsandsociety.org/article.php?id=386).

Cornell University. "Genetically Engineered Organisms, Public Issues Education Project." Retrieved February 12, 2008 (http://www.geo-pie.cornell.edu/crops/eating.html).

GMO Compass. "Breeding Aims: Disease Resistance." Retrieved February 13, 2008 (http://www.gmo-compass.org/eng/agri_biotechnology/breeding_aims/148.disease_resistant_crops.html).

GMO Compass. "Breeding Aims: Production of Pharmaceuticals, Enzymes, and 'Bio' Raw Materials." Retrieved February 13, 2008 (http://www.gmo-compass.org/eng/agri_biotechnology/breeding_aims/150.pharming.html).

Heller, Lorraine. "FDA Sued for Lax Regulation of GM Foods." Food Navigator-USA, June 9, 2006. Retrieved February 21, 2008 (http://www.foodnavigator-usa.com/news/ng.asp?n=68312-cfs-fda-ge-gm).

Henkel, John. "Genetic Engineering: Fast Forwarding to Future Foods." *FDA Consumer*, February 1998. Retrieved February 12, 2008 (http://www.fda.gov/bbs/topics/CONSUMER/geneng.html).

International Service for the Acquisition of Agri-Biotech Applications. "Global Status of Commercialized Biotech/ GM Crops 2007." Brief 37-2007. Retrieved February 12, 2008 (http://www.isaaa.org/resources/publications/briefs/37/ executivesummary/default.html).

Lambrecht, Bill. *Dinner at the New Gene Café*. New York, NY: St. Martin's, 2001.

The Royal Society. "The Use of Genetically Modified Animals." May 2001. Retrieved February 21, 2008 (http://royalsociety. org/displaypagedoc.asp?id=11513).

Tegene, Abebayehu, Wallace E. Huffman, Matthew Rousu, and Jason S. Shogren. "The Effects of Information on Consumer Demand for Biotech Foods: Evidence from Experimental Auctions." Technical Publication 1903, *ERS Briefs*. Washington, DC: U.S. Department of Agriculture, 2003.

Thomson, Jennifer A. *Seeds for the Future*. New York, NY: Cornell University Press, 2006.

INDEX

A

allergies, 44–45, 47
American Association for Laboratory Science, 38
animal welfare, 36–38
antibiotic resistance, 23, 44
antioxidants, 49–50

B

bacteria
  Agrobacterium tumefaciens, 22
  Bacillus thuringiensis (Bt), 26, 35
Bateson, William, 13
biodiversity, 5, 26–27, 35–36
biolistics, 22

C

Calgene, 15
Canadian regulatory agencies, 46–47
cancer, 16, 37, 49
canola oil, 21, 48
Center for Food Safety, 46
chickens, 4, 38
cloning, 13, 17
corn, 4, 8, 21, 26, 35, 48, 51
Correns, Carl Erich, 13
cows, 4, 8, 10, 17, 18
Crop and Food Research, 50
cross-fertilization, 10

D

diabetes, 37

Dolly the sheep, 17–18
drought, 36

E

Edler, Eric, 13
environment, 5, 15, 26, 27, 45, 50
Environmental Protection Agency (EPA), 45
European Union, 47

F

Flavr Savr Tomato, 15–16
Food and Drug Administration (FDA), 15, 17, 45–46
  and 2006 lawsuit, 46

G

gene, word origin of, 9, 13
gene gun, 22
genetic engineering, 4, 13, 18, 50
genetic modification
  definition of, 4, 6–8
  early history of, 8–11
  effects on animal health, 5, 17–18, 30–31, 36–37
  effects on human health, 5, 27, 31–32, 38, 43–44
  effects on nonmodified organisms, 33–35
  methods of, 19–24
  myths about, 51
  regulation of, 44, 45–48
golden rice, 32

About the Author

Jeri Freedman earned a B.A. degree from Harvard University. For fifteen years, she worked for companies in the medical field. Among the numerous books she has written for young adults are *The Human Population and the Nitrogen Cycle*, *Hemophilia*, *Hepatitis B*, *Lymphoma: Current and Emerging Trends in Detection and Treatment*, *How Do We Know About Genetics and Heredity?*, *The Mental and Physical Effects of Obesity*, *Autism*, and *Tay-Sachs Disease*.

Photo Credits

Cover, pp. 7, 17, 28 courtesy of USDA/ARS, photo by Scott Bauer; cover (bottom inset) © www.istockphoto.com/Mara Radeva; cover and interior background and decorative elements © www.istockphoto.com/Sebastian Kaulitzki, © www.istockphoto.com/Yuri Khristich, © www.istockphoto.com/appleuzr, © www.istockphoto.com/marc brown, © www.istockphoto.com/bigredlynx; pp. 5, 31 David Greedy/Getty Images; p. 9 © Shelia Terry/Photo Researchers, Inc.; pp. 11, 24 courtesy of USDA/ARS, photo by Peggy Greb; p. 12 Authenticated News/Hulton Archive/Getty Images; p. 14 © Rosenfeld Images, Ltd./Photo Researchers, Inc.; p. 16 pttmedical/Newscom; p. 20 Toru Yamanaka/AFP/Getty Images; p. 23 © SciMAT/Photo Researchers, Inc.; p. 26 David McNew/Getty Images; p. 30 Choi Seng-Sik/AFP/Getty Images; pp. 34, 42, 49 © AP Images; p. 36 © Peter Menzel/Photo Researchers, Inc.; p. 38 courtesy of USDA/ARS, photo by Stephen Ausmus; p. 45 © Voisin/Phanie/Photo Researchers, Inc.; p. 48 © Robert Brook/Photo Researchers, Inc.

Designer: Evelyn Horovicz; Cover Designer: Nelson Sá
Editor: Kathy Kuhtz Campbell